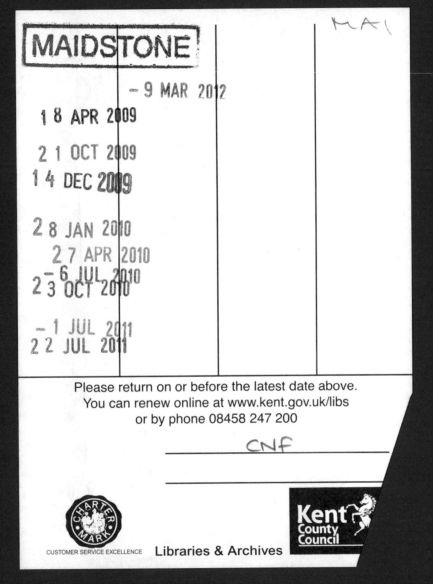

HISTORY IN ART

VICTORIAN BRITAIN

Raintree

ANDREW LANGLEY

www.raintreepublishers.co.uk
Visit our website to find out more information about **Raintree** books.

To order:
☎ Phone 44 (0) 1865 888112
🖷 Send a fax to 44 (0) 1865 314091
🖥 Visit the Raintree Bookshop at **www.raintreepublishers.co.uk** to browse our catalogue and order online.

Produced for Raintree by
White-Thomson Publishing Ltd
Bridgewater Business Centre, 210 High Street,
Lewes, East Sussex, BN7 2NH.

First published in Great Britain by Raintree, Halley Court,
Jordan Hill, Oxford OX2 8EJ, part of Harcourt Education.
Raintree is a registered trademark of Harcourt Education Ltd.

Editorial: Cath Senker and Diyan Leake
Consultant: Dr Michael Partridge, St Mary's College, Twickenham
Design: Richard Parker
Page make-up: Mind's Eye Design Ltd, Lewes
Picture research: Elaine Fuoco-Lang
Map artwork: Encompass Graphics
Production: Kevin Blackman
Originated by Dot Gradations
Printed and bound in Hong Kong, China
by South China Printing Company

ISBN 1 844 43373 0
09 08 07 06 05
10 9 8 7 6 5 4 3 2 1

British Library Cataloguing in Publication Data
Langley, Andrew
History in Art: Victorian Britain
709.4'1'09034
A full catalogue record for this book is available from the
British Library.

Acknowledgements
The publishers would like to thank the following for permission
to reproduce photographs (t = top, b = bottom): The Advertising
Archive p. **29** (t); Art Archive **contents page** (Victoria and Albert
Museum/Eileen Tweedy), pp. **5** (t) (Julia Margaret Cameron), **7** (b)
(Tate Gallery London/Eileen Tweedy), **8** (Miramare Museum
Trieste/Dagli Orti), **9** (t) (British Museum/ Eileen Tweedy), **10**,
11 (t), **12** (Bibliothèque des Arts Décoratifs, Paris/Dagli Orti),
13 (t), **14** (Victoria and Albert Museum/Eileen Tweedy), **15** (t)
(Bibliothèque des Arts Décoratifs, Paris/Dagli Orti), **16** (Victoria
and Albert Museum/Eileen Tweedy), **17** (b) (Bibliothèque des Arts
Décoratifs, Paris/Dagli Orti), **18**, **20** (Dagli Orti), **22**, **23**, **25** (t)
(RAMC Historical Museum/Harper Collins Publishers), **26** (Dagli
Orti), **27** (t), **29** (b) (Eileen Tweedy), **30** (Victoria and Albert
Museum/Sally Chappell), **31** (Victoria and Albert Museum/Sally
Chappell), **33** (t) (Victoria and Albert Museum London/Sally Chappell),
34 (Christies/Eileen Tweedy), **35** (Russell Cotes Art Gallery/Eileen
Tweedy), **41** (t) (Tate Gallery/Eileen Tweedy), **41** (b), **43** (t), **45**
(Bibliothèque des Arts Décoratifs, Paris/Dagli Orti); Bridgeman pp. **7**
(t), **9** (b), **13** (b), **15** (b), **17** (t), **19** (both), **21**, **32** (Manchester Art
Gallery), **33** (b), **36** (Manchester Art Gallery), **39**, **40**, **42**; Corbis pp.
25 (b) (Angelo Hornak), **37** (left) (Robert Holmes); Chris Fairclough
p. **5** (b); Mary Evans Picture Library pp. **24**, **27** (b); Maynooth College
pp. **6**, **44**; National Trust Photographic Library p. **28** (Rupert Truman);
Oldham Art Gallery p. **38**; Tate Gallery p. **37** (right); Travelsite pp. **11** (b)
(Neil Setchfield), **43** (b) (Neil Setchfield). Cover photograph of part of
a bronze sculpture by Alfred Drury (1857–1954) reproduced with
permission of Bridgeman Art Library (The Maas Gallery, London, UK).

Contents

Words included in the glossary are in **bold** the first time they appear in each chapter.

Victorian art

The Victorian era stretched for most of the 19th century. Born in 1819, Queen Victoria came to the throne in 1837 while still a teenager and ruled for over 63 years, until she died in 1901. This was an amazingly energetic and inventive age.

The Victorian period saw Britain reach the pinnacle of its economic power, and expand its empire across the world. Yet it was also an age of widespread poverty, when industrial **pollution** and urban growth began to do serious harm to the environment.

What's left of the Victorians?

Victorian culture is all around us, most obviously in architecture. Some of the best-known buildings in the land, from the Houses of Parliament to Tower Bridge, were designed by Victorians. Many big cities, such as Leeds and Manchester, boast grand and ornate Victorian town halls and museums. Almost every town has Victorian schools and churches, along with terraces of Victorian houses.

All of these buildings tell us a lot about the taste and technical skills of the period, as well as its huge wealth and self-confidence. We can learn more about how the Victorians lived and what they thought from the paintings, carvings, ceramics (objects made from

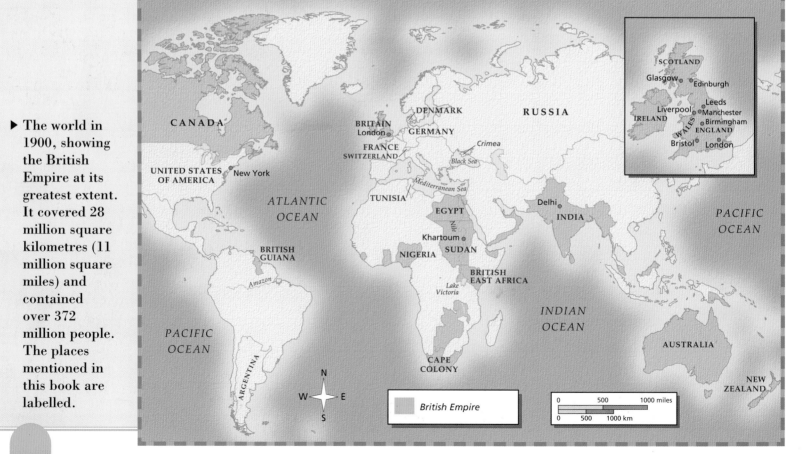

▶ The world in 1900, showing the British Empire at its greatest extent. It covered 28 million square kilometres (11 million square miles) and contained over 372 million people. The places mentioned in this book are labelled.

clay) and other objects inside the museums, galleries and country houses of the time. They were the first people to be captured in photographs, a brand-new art form at the time. This was also the greatest age of fiction writing in Britain. Novelists such as Charles Dickens, Elizabeth Gaskell, George Eliot and Thomas Hardy give us a wonderfully vivid picture of Victorian society, describing rich and poor in town and country.

The Victorian influence

The artistic style of the Victorians soon fell out of favour. By the end of the Second World War in 1945, the British Empire was shrinking and the influence of Christianity was declining. No one wanted high-minded pictures of heroic soldiers or grieving widows any longer. Public knowledge about the era decreased so much that in 1958 the Victorian Society was founded in London by the poet John Betjeman and others, to study and protect buildings and art of the period. Since then, interest in Victorian culture has soared, and many artists, designers and architects have been deeply influenced by it.

▼ The Houses of Parliament on the banks of the Thames at Westminster in London. The previous parliament building had burned down.

▼ *The Angel at the Sepulchre*, a photograph by Julia Margaret Cameron from 1870. Although she took portrait photographs of celebrities such as Lord Tennyson and Charles Darwin, she also created mystical shots like this, using the camera to reflect the subject's inner spirit.

The dreamy expression on the model's face echoes the paintings of the **Pre-Raphaelites**

The heavy drapes are carefully folded to give a gloomy romantic air

The camera is very close up to the model's face, which is brightly lit

The Houses of Parliament

Early Victorian architects looked to the past for inspiration. In 1835 a competition was held to design the new Houses of Parliament in London. The winner was Charles Barry (helped by Augustus Pugin), and his plan was a triumph for what is called the **Gothic Revival**. This style involved copying the features of great medieval architecture, with towers, spires, pointed arches, stained glass and highly detailed decoration. The huge structure was not completed until 1867.

Examining the evidence

Victorian Britain is never very far away. Most railway journeys take us along routes, through tunnels and over bridges built in the 19th century. Victorian factory buildings still dominate parts of the urban landscape. The art of the period is even closer. Many people live in Victorian houses, with furniture and interior decoration copied from the period. We can even buy examples of Victorian art from antique shops and market stalls and study them at home.

▼ St Patrick's College in Maynooth, Ireland, is a seminary for men studying to be Roman Catholic priests. The extensive structure, built between 1846 and 1853, was designed by Augustus Welby Pugin, an early champion of the Gothic Revival in architecture.

What can art tell us?

All of these things, together with the vast quantity of other work produced by artists and architects, form a rich source of evidence about how the Victorians lived and worked, and what they believed in. Of course, there are many other ways of finding out about the period, through the books, public records, newspapers and letters of the time. Photography and sound recordings are a good source too. For example, there is a recording of the poet Alfred Tennyson reading his poem *The Charge of the Light Brigade*, about the Crimean War.

Art makes excellent source material because it is easily accessible. Pictures and buildings are there to be looked at and closely examined.

Decoration is kept simple, without the ornate decoration of the Houses of Parliament, for example

The entrance gate echoes the gatehouse of a medieval castle

Round towers with pointed roofs, in imitation of French Gothic castles

The cottage parlour contains little furniture, but is very clean

Granny comes in at the front door, carrying a basket and doll for the children

A toddler runs to greet her

A well-fed and contented baby sleeps in its basket

◄ George Smith's charming painting called *Here's Granny*. This is typical of dozens of Victorian rural pictures, with its cosy cottage interior and well-scrubbed characters.

The mother sits in front of the hearth with her sewing

Victorian paintings cover an enormous variety of subjects, from village scenes and Highland stags to noble families and social gatherings. They give us a bright and lively impression of Britain in the 19th century. First of all, however, the right questions have to be asked. How were these things made? Who created them and who bought them?

Painters and patrons

The Victorian period was an era of peace at home and growing prosperity for many. Producing goods such as cotton and **steel** brought wealth to **manufacturers** and merchants, and these people formed a new rich **middle class**. They could afford to live and eat well, and to pay for comfortable new houses. Many were also eager to buy art for their homes – not the works of Old Masters (painters of the 17th and 18th centuries), but new painting and sculpture.

As a result, some fashionable artists became extremely rich and famous. Painters such as Lord Frederic Leighton and Lawrence Alma-Tadema were celebrities, with luxurious homes and grand studios. Even artists who were less successful had a good chance of making a living, thanks to the opening of many new galleries (including London's National Gallery in 1838), and the work of art dealers and agents.

▶ John Singer Sargent's painting *Carnation, Lily, Lily, Rose* (1886) is another and even more idealized picture of children, this time in a middle-class setting. Two girls in pretty dresses stand with lanterns amid the bright colours of a flower garden.

Examining the evidence

Middle-class people wanted paintings that reflected their own values, concentrating on innocent childhood, family life, and uplifting moral messages. Many pictures contain comfortable and reassuring images that, like this one, harked back to an idyllic rural past.

The Victorian story

Victoria came to the throne at a difficult time. The British were unhappy with their rulers, following the reigns of the scandalous George IV and the weak-willed William IV. Parliament now had a much greater role in running the country, and the monarch was becoming more of a symbol than a powerful ruler.

'Two nations'

Britain was a deeply divided society. Government was still in the hands of the wealthy upper classes. At the start of Victoria's reign, only about 20 per cent of men (and no women) were allowed to vote in general elections. In 1838 the **Chartist** Movement was founded. Its members demonstrated and presented **petitions** demanding that all men should be able to vote.

At this time, huge numbers of poor people in the rapidly growing industrial towns could scarcely afford even to eat. In Manchester and Liverpool alone, over 80,000 people lived in cellars, and many existed on coffee and bread alone.

Early Victorian paintings rarely reflect this bitter division. It was the novelists who examined the unpleasant realities of poverty, disease and appalling working conditions. In 1845, a young politician called Benjamin Disraeli published *Sybil*, in which he described rich and poor as the 'two nations' of Britain. Charles Dickens wrote a string of hugely popular novels about all classes of society, which drew attention to the despair in which many people lived.

▼ This **engraved** portrait of Queen Victoria is by an unknown artist. It shows the queen in 1855 when she was 36 years old.

Victoria wears a tiara, typically worn by aristocratic ladies

The artist has shown Victoria's darkened eyes – something that you can see in others of her family

The queen's chin looks more pronounced than it does in other portraits

She holds a paper in her hand to show that she is involved in state matters

▶ The young Oliver meets Fagin, the head of a gang of thieves, in this illustration from Charles Dickens's sensational bestselling novel *Oliver Twist*, published as a serial in 1837–38. The artist was George Cruikshank.

At the same time, the country was being transformed by major developments in industry and transport. Towns were expanding fast as houses were built for the workers employed in the new factories, cotton mills and iron foundries. Railway lines were being laid across Britain, giving people the chance to travel further and faster than they had ever done before. Farming was flourishing too, providing food for the expanding population.

Victoria and Albert

'Poor little Queen!' wrote Thomas Carlyle after Victoria's coronation in 1838. But the eighteen-year-old quickly showed that she was strong and determined enough to cope with the massive responsibility. She was helped first of all by the Prime Minister, Lord Melbourne, who gave wise and fatherly advice. (Her own father had died when she was a baby.) Then, in 1840, she married her German cousin Prince Albert. It was a happy marriage, and gave Victoria a stability and confidence lacking in her own childhood.

Fagin stands with a toasting fork, cooking sausages over a fire

A washing line, draped with the silk handkerchiefs stolen by Fagin's gang

Fagin's boys sit around the table smoking long pipes and drinking

The 'Artful Dodger', who has befriended Oliver and brought him back

Oliver Twist (who had run away from his previous home) clutches his bundle of belongings

▶ A dramatic oil painting of Queen Victoria riding in Windsor Great Park near London in 1865, by Sir Edwin Landseer. The queen is shown as a commanding figure, riding side-saddle on horseback. As always, Landseer was keen to put in as many animals as possible alongside his main subject – including a hound and a dead stag.

Royal portraits

Kings and queens had always used art to project images of strength and authority. There are many such 'official' portraits of the young Victoria, showing her wearing state robes, seated on the throne or meeting her Privy Council (the most important ministers and advisers). In spite of her grand surroundings, the artists often portray her as young, uneasy and vulnerable. Later portraits of her married life with Prince Albert (such as Edwin Landseer's *Windsor Castle in Modern Times*) show a more relaxed and contented figure.

War and empire

War had been a central part of European history for centuries. However, following the Battle of Waterloo in 1815, most of the continent enjoyed a long period of peace. At the same time, Britain was building up an empire of overseas **colonies**. By 1850 it included Canada, India, Ireland, Australia, New Zealand and much of modern-day South Africa. These vast areas brought in wealth through trade, but large amounts of money and large numbers of people were required to administer and control them.

▼ The Charge of the Light Brigade in the Crimean War, as depicted in an engraving from the original painting by R. Caton Woodville. It was a tragic mistake, in which the cavalry were ordered to charge the wrong battery of guns. Nearly 120 out of 661 men were killed (as well as 362 horses), but the charge was recalled as a stirring example of gallantry and daring. The incident took place in 1854, yet this picture was still immensely popular over 40 years later.

The Crimean War

In 1853, Britain, France and other countries joined forces to stop Russia from expanding its frontiers in Crimea, near the Black Sea. Russia was defeated but the Crimean War highlighted worrying faults in the organization of the British army. During the winter of 1854–55 the troops had to suffer terrible conditions, with little shelter from the bad weather. They had poor equipment, and inadequate food and medical supplies. Thousands died of disease and cold as well as from battle wounds.

This was the first major conflict in history to be recorded in photographs (photography had been invented in England and France in 1839). The official painters produced heroic and patriotic scenes, glorifying the Charge of the Light Brigade and the stand of the 93rd Highlanders at Balaclava (both 1854). In contrast, photographs showed the snow and mud, the tattered uniforms and the ill-fed and stressed faces of the troops.

Led by Lord Cardigan, the Light Brigade rides towards the Russian guns

They are armed with sabres

The cavalrymen are shown with perfect and colourful uniforms

◀ The interior of a peasant family's cabin in Ireland during the famine of 1845–46. It was painted by Erskine Nicol, a Scottish artist who lived in Ireland. Some of his other pictures show the comic side of Irish life.

We can only see two faces full on, and both look grim and hopeless

The timber dwelling has bare walls and a beaten earth floor

Famine and rebellion

The military sufferings in the Crimea were mild compared to the tragedy of the Irish famine. The failures of the vital potato crop in Ireland in 1845 and 1846 led to mass starvation. Nearly a million people died, and by 1860 another two million had fled the country to settle in North America. The British authorities were slow to help. A secret society called the Fenian Brotherhood was formed in 1859 to fight for independence from Britain. It began a series of terrorist actions, including an attack on Chester Castle and the blowing up of a London prison in 1867.

Much further from home, there was appalling bloodshed in India. In 1857 three regiments of Indian troops mutinied (rebelled) against their British rulers. The revolt swiftly spread through Delhi and central India, and hundreds of Europeans were killed. The British regained control a year later, but their revenge was savage. In a storm of looting and massacre — which the Indians called 'The Devil's Wind' — they slaughtered just as many as the rebels had done.

▶ The bronze statue of Prince Albert (with the catalogue of the Great Exhibition in his hand) is the focus of the huge Albert Memorial in London. It was created by John Foley in 1876.

The death of Albert

The happiest period of Queen Victoria's life ended in 1861 with the death of Prince Albert. Shattered by the loss, she withdrew from public life for many years, spending much of her time away from London at Balmoral, her Scottish home, or at Osborne House on the Isle of Wight. She had an ornate tomb built for Albert (and herself) in Windsor Park, and ordered the creation of the Albert Memorial in Hyde Park, London.

The struggle for reform

Reform was desperately needed in the 19th century. Throughout Queen Victoria's long life, campaigners fought to gain improved conditions in factories, prisons, schools, the armed forces and urban **slums**. The explosive growth in the population had created new problems, especially for the poor. They (and their children) worked long hours in unhealthy and dangerous places, and went home to bad housing, unclean water and not enough food.

Reforming the law

Very slowly, the government passed laws to improve people's working lives. In 1847 the 'Ten-Hour' Act limited women and children to ten hours' work a day. (They still worked 58 hours a week!) New safety rules for coal mines were introduced in 1850. In 1853 a new criminal law meant convicts (people in prison) could no longer be sent overseas. Further Reform Acts in 1867 and 1884 allowed most men – though still no women – to vote. Local authorities were forced to employ inspectors to keep a check on public health and drinking water.

Meanwhile, others outside parliament made their own efforts to help the poor. In 1862 George Peabody, an American millionaire, founded an organization to build better working-class housing in London. Thomas Barnado opened his first home for orphan children in 1867. The very first congress (meeting) of the **trade unions**, representing ... k place in 1868. In 1878, ... blished the Salvation Army ... d shelter for the homeless.

▼A seamstress at work, in an engraving from 1854. Women such as this laboured long hours alone for very little pay.

Basket containing reels of cotton

Pincushion

The surroundings are bare but spacious; the details of poverty are not shown

Hard work with needle and thread often damaged the worker's fingers and hands

The woman is depicted as modest and dignified, despite the humble nature of her work

▶ Inhabitants of a slum area in Glasgow assemble for the camera (with their washing) in 1868. Photographs showed real social conditions much more starkly than engravings, but there was no method at this time for printing them in magazines.

Pictures for printing

The *Illustrated London News*, founded in 1842, was the world's first illustrated newspaper. It was followed by the weekly *Graphic* in 1869. Photographs could not be reproduced cheaply, so articles were accompanied by engravings – illustrations printed from engraved blocks. Many of the artists employed by these papers produced memorable scenes of life among the poor and distressed.

Realistic paintings

Most of our images of poverty, hardship and slum life come from Victorian paintings. The most hard-hitting pictures are works of the later part of the period. During the first half of Queen Victoria's reign, most painters thought that factory scenes and poor people were not suitable subjects for art. The few pictures that did show poverty usually left out the grimmer details. For example, Richard Redgrave's *The Sempstress* portrays the lonely needlewoman as an almost saintly figure, suffering but dignified.

It was only in the 1870s that a more **realistic** style appeared. The painting *Applicants for Admission to a Casual Ward* showed homeless people queueing outside

a hostel. By using dark and dull colours, and exaggerating the despair in the faces, the artist created a dramatic effect. The French illustrator Gustave Doré made a series of shocking studies of scenes in the London slums. Other pictures revealed the hardships of rural life, such as Henry Wallis's portrait of a dead **stonebreaker**.

▼*Applicants for Admission to a Casual Ward* by Samuel Luke Fildes (1874). The image originally appeared as a small black-and-white engraving in *Graphic* magazine, under the title *Houseless and Hungry*. Fildes later painted it in oils on a canvas nearly 3 metres high.

The dingy colours add to the atmosphere of despair and misery

A policeman directs a newcomer to the queue

Nearly all the poor people in the painting have their heads bent down

The queue of homeless people waits outside an overnight refuge

Many of the children have fallen asleep on their feet

End of an era

On the face of it, Britain in the 1880s was successful economically. Prices in the shops were falling, and the number of people in work was rising. The empire was about to reach its peak, giving the country better trading opportunities than any other nation. Nevertheless, there were major problems. One was how to cope with the population, which had risen from 17 million in 1837 to 34 million in 1875. Another was the growing economic strength of other countries, especially the USA and Germany.

Troubles at home and abroad

As Queen Victoria reached old age, the problems grew worse. The strains of controlling the vast British Empire, which covered one-fifth of the Earth's land mass, were beginning to tell. Since 1880, European powers had rushed to grab land in Africa, and among Britain's new colonies were British East Africa, Nigeria and Egypt. British troops often struggled to control these territories. Their most bloody war took place in Egypt and the Sudan, where rebels wiped out a **garrison** of soldiers at Khartoum.

At the same time, unrest was reaching a peak in Ireland. In 1882, terrorists murdered Lord Frederick Cavendish, the Chief Secretary for Ireland, in the capital, Dublin. Campaigners for and against **Home Rule** (independence from Britain) staged a series of riots across the country. The sense of gloom deepened in England too, when a survey showed that one Londoner in three lived in great poverty. The growing power of the trade unions was shown by two major industrial strikes, by the London dockers in 1889, and the coal miners in 1893.

Caricatures aimed to convey the subject's character by exaggerating some features; in this case, the head is on a bigger scale than the body

The artist stresses Gladstone's earnest and humourless personality – he is lined and there is no sign of a smile

◀ William Ewart Gladstone was one of the most famous politicians of the Victorian era, serving as Prime Minister four times between 1868 and 1894. This caricature picture of him was the work of an artist who used the nickname *Singe* (French for 'monkey').

▶ Queen Victoria in 1886, the year before her Golden Jubilee. The portrait is an engraved copy of a photograph taken by Alexander Bassano.

The coronet, or small-sized crown, is worn with a lace headdress

Victoria's jubilees

The queen's long period of retirement had ended in 1887 when she passed through the streets of London to a thanksgiving service for her Golden Jubilee (celebrating 50 years on the throne). There were even greater celebrations a decade later, when Victoria's Diamond Jubilee procession took place. It was swelled by 50,000 soldiers from all parts of the empire. Huge crowds gathered to cheer the old lady who had given them a feeling of stability in difficult times.

She still missed Albert dreadfully. 'I sat alone,' she wrote, 'Oh! Without my beloved husband!' Her children had all married, and several had made powerful matches with European royal families. The British monarchy had forged strong connections with Denmark, Russia, Prussia, and newly formed Germany after 1871. When Victoria died in 1901, the crown passed to her eldest son, who became Edward VII.

Victoria is sitting in a stiff and formal manner, emphasizing her royal authority

Late Victorian art

In 1877 the art critic John Ruskin attacked a new painting by the artist James McNeill Whistler, called *Nocturne in Black and Gold*. He clearly did not understand Whistler's daring and almost **abstract** style, and likened it to 'flinging a pot of paint in the public's face'. Whistler was one of the **pioneers** of a new kind of painting, which was greatly influenced by the French **Impressionists**. Among his followers were Walter Sickert and Philip Wilson Steer.

◀ One of the most controversial paintings of the age – James McNeill Whistler's *Nocturne in Black and Gold: the Falling Rocket.*

The age of industry

When Victoria came to the throne, goods worth £44 million were being exported (sold abroad) each year. By 1880 that figure had shot up to £218 million. Mills turned raw cotton from North America into cloth, blast furnaces turned iron ore into iron and **steel**, and mines produced vast supplies of coal.

There were factories with machines making everything from bridges and ships to screws and tools. Huge numbers of people spent their lives operating these machines. (There were more than a million **textile** workers alone in the 1850s.) This huge development of industry, which had started in the eighteenth century, was known as the industrial revolution.

Picturing workers

One of the most famous images of industrial Britain is *Iron and Coal*, painted by William Bell Scott in 1861. It depicts a metal-working shop, possibly part of a shipbuilding yard, on Tyneside, with three hefty and heroic-looking workers wielding sledgehammers. A forge fire glows, and in the background a massive bridge and the masts of ships can be seen. Scott's picture is clearly not meant to be realistic, but to illustrate the nobility of the working man as a vital part of British industry.

Painters tended to be interested in the dramatic effects inside factories. They showed the glare and smoke of blast furnaces, the manly muscles of the workers, and the grand scale of processes such as pouring molten iron or lifting enormous weights. More realistic scenes of the industrial landscape were drawn for magazines or newspapers, as in the nightmarish **engraving** of factories near Wolverhampton in 1866. Photographs, too, conveyed images of real bleakness.

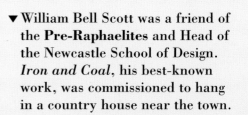

▼ William Bell Scott was a friend of the **Pre-Raphaelites** and Head of the Newcastle School of Design. *Iron and Coal*, his best-known work, was commissioned to hang in a country house near the town.

Shipping on the River Tyne in the background

The stylized (not realistic) design of the painting can be seen in the neat arrangement of the three raised hammers

Chains and pulley system for lifting iron ship parts

This woman is sitting dangerously close to the action and the forge!

The workers are hammering on a piece of molten metal as it emerges from the furnace

Life in a cotton mill

People flocked from the country to the towns to find factory work. Their reward might have been a career in a Lancashire cotton mill. In the 1840s this would have meant a working week of twelve hours a day from Monday to Friday and nine hours on Saturday. There was an hour's break at midday, but little other time off. Anyone who was late or failed to keep up with the machines might be fined or sacked.

Cotton mills were not as dangerous as mines or foundries, but were far from healthy. Germs flourished in the damp, warm atmosphere, and many workers contracted lung disease from breathing in cotton fibres. Metal shops, potteries and match factories had their own forms of **pollution**. On top of this was the threat of accidents – workers' limbs could get caught in the machinery. Few machines had safety guards in the first part of the century.

▶ A graphic illustration of the workers' struggle for basic rights: a 19th-century banner of the Southend-on-Sea branch of the National Union of Railwaymen.

Trade union banners

By the 1830s workers had gained the legal right to form unions, which gave them greater power to demand better working conditions and wages. Many associations sprang up, but it was not until 1851 that the first modern **trade union** was established – the Amalgamated Society of Engineers. Other national unions were also founded. Each one represented a section of industry and had its own special banner for parades and demonstrations.

The forest of chimneys fills the sky with black smoke and other dangerous fumes

Vast heaps of waste products tower over the buildings – these are slag heaps

◀ The massive pollution caused by uncontrolled industrial growth is made dramatically clear in this engraving. It is a view of Vivian's copper foundry at Swansea in Wales, surrounded by dozens more factories and forges.

Sailing vessels bring raw materials and carry away the forged metal products

The river is polluted with chemical spillage from the copper works

Steam and speed

The power of steam had been a crucial factor in the industrial age since the early 1700s. Steam engines had pumped water out of mines, turned **lathes** and drills, threshed corn and driven spinning machines. Yet the most revolutionary effect of steam was seen in the 1820s, when the first passenger railways were opened. By the time Victoria became queen, Britain was in the grip of 'railway mania', which saw the building of a network of lines across the country. Many paintings reflect the way that trains changed travelling conditions and the landscape itself.

Faster than a horse

J. M. W. Turner's 1844 painting called *Rain, Steam and Speed* is one of the most famous British works of art.

Subtitled *The Great Western Railway*, it shows a glowing steam locomotive hurtling across a viaduct through swirls of misty rain, like a fiery monster. The novelist William Thackeray wrote 'The world has never seen anything like this picture.'

People today are used to seeing huge machines in action, and to travelling at great speeds. But these things were still amazing to the Victorians. Throughout history, the fastest anyone could move was on the back of a galloping horse. Now, steam trains could whisk you along at 70 kilometres an hour (40 miles an hour) – or even quicker. In 1904, the steam engine *City of Truro* reached 160 kilometres an hour (100 miles an hour). Turner's painting celebrates the raw and apparently unstoppable energy of the machine.

▶ The vitality and power of the industrial revolution is conveyed in J.M.W. Turner's *Rain, Steam and Speed – The Great Western Railway*.

The slanting rain adds to the impression of wildness and extreme speed

The boat on the River Thames seems slow and old fashioned compared with the train

Young girls dance on the riverbank, representing the more innocent way of life before the industrial age

The steam locomotive rushes towards the viewer across the viaduct

A tiny hare runs in front of the locomotive, symbolizing natural energy

Travelling by train

Steam railways changed the way many people lived. They could now travel between most places (in England at least) in a single day. There were no overnight stops, so it was cheaper than a coach as well as much faster and more comfortable. The coach journey from London to Glasgow took 42 hours; by rail, it took only 12 hours. For the first time, ordinary people could take holidays far from home, and railway companies ran special 'excursion' trains to seaside resorts.

Rail travel fascinated many artists. There are several well-known paintings of train interiors, including Augustus Egg's *Travelling Companions* and Abraham Solomon's *The Meeting*, showing a chance encounter in a first-class carriage. Some pictures were sensationally popular, such as William Powell Frith's bustling 1862 panorama of Paddington Station in London, *The Railway Station*. Huge crowds came to see it on exhibition, and the scene was even imitated on stage as part of a play.

▶ Two emigrants leave their native land on board a ship bound for a new life in North America. Ford Madox Brown's famous picture *The Last of England* (1860) conveys the uncertainty of the voyage.

Steam at sea

Steam was also used to power ships, making them faster than sailing ships and not dependent on winds and tides. By the 1850s, thousands of Britons were using the steamships to move to the USA and parts of the empire as far away as Australia. Their experience was captured in poignant paintings such as Ford Madox Brown's *The Last of England*. But the grandness and elegance of first-class steamship travel also provided material for society painters such as James Tissot.

▶ William Powell Frith's *The Railway Station* was a large painting packed with figures and activity. When it was first shown at a private gallery in London in 1862, it attracted 21,000 visitors in seven weeks.

For the hurrying passengers, Frith used professional models who posed in his studio and he also made many sketches on the spot

The great covered 'shed' at Paddington Station, designed by Isambard Kingdom Brunel. Frith had had professional photographs of the background taken so that he could paint from them

The huge crowd contains passengers from all classes of society – a sign of the wide appeal of the railways

Industrial beauty

The Victorians transformed their world. They built structures bigger and bolder than anything since the great cathedrals of the Middle Ages. Their bridges, factories, ships, pumping stations and machines were made for commercial rather than religious reasons, but they were often things of great beauty. So we can look at them as partly artistic creations, and examine what they tell us about the 19th century's age of industry.

Railways and bridges

The Victorian age produced dozens of brilliant railway engineers and architects, such as Robert Stephenson, W. H. Barlow and Isambard Kingdom Brunel. The colourful and ruthless Brunel was the mastermind behind the Great Western Railway which linked London to the West Country. He not only planned the route but also designed everything from tunnels and station buildings to carriages and staff uniforms. His finest works include the bridges at Maidenhead and Clifton Gorge, the giant steamship *Great Eastern,* and the canopy at Paddington Station.

These vast schemes needed armies of workers to build them. In 1846, at the height of the railway-building mania, there were more than 200,000 'navvies' (short for 'navigators') throughout Britain. Their work rate was incredible. With little more than picks, shovels and wheelbarrows, plus a little gunpowder, they dug cuttings and tunnels, raised embankments (walls of earth) and built bridges, changing the appearance of the landscape.

Three massive cantilevers (giant brackets) reached out across the two main spans

The girders joined the cantilevers together

▼ Many great Victorian structures were beautiful to look at. The Forth Bridge, built between 1882 and 1889, carried the railway for nearly two kilometres across the Firth of Forth. It used over 54,000 tonnes of steel.

The cantilevers 'gave' (expanded and contracted) naturally under the regular weight of trains

The bridge contains 59 hectares of metal, which has had to be regularly painted ever since

Supporting brick piers underneath

The power of the photograph

Before the Victorian age, the only images of famous people had been portrait paintings. The invention of photography changed that. Our impressions of great personalities of the period – Victoria herself, Florence Nightingale or the politician William Gladstone – are gained from photographs instead of portraits. Few photographs express the character of their subject better than this celebrated picture of Brunel standing in front of the *Great Eastern* before its launch in 1857.

▶ Isambard Kingdom Brunel stands in front of the vast chains used to launch his biggest ship, the *Great Eastern*, in 1857. This photograph conveys the personality of the man – determined, focused and not at all self-conscious. In placing man against machinery it also expresses the boundless confidence of Victorian engineering.

Power and pride

What do we learn about the Victorian engineers from the style and scale of these great structures? Clearly, they express a feeling of enormous confidence and ambition. It was felt that technology could be used to solve all kinds of problems. When someone suggested to Brunel that his railway was too long, he replied, 'Why not make it longer – and have a steamboat go from Bristol to New York?' This confidence can be seen in grand projects like St Pancras station in London (completed in 1874) and the Forth Bridge (opened in 1890).

Victorian engineers took pride in their ability to make their buildings graceful and pleasing to the eye. Factories, warehouses and banks were highly decorated and designed to look grand. Even humble places such as water pumping stations could be made to look like classical temples. Whitacre Pumping Station in Staffordshire, for example, featured ornate iron columns and friezes (decorated borders on the upper part of a wall), topped with gilded corbels (supports or brackets) in the shape of eagles.

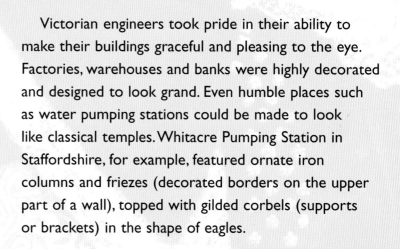

Many inventions

In May 1851 Queen Victoria opened the Great Exhibition, housed in the brand-new Crystal Palace in London's Hyde Park. Devised by her beloved husband Albert, the exhibition celebrated the marvellous machines and other inventions of the age. Most of the exhibits were British, but others came from as far away as Tunisia and Russia. In the next few months, over six million people packed in to examine the 13,000 exhibits, which included steam coaches, Swiss watches, gas cookers, turnip washers and even a model of a floating church for the use of sailors.

▼ Joseph Paxton's Crystal Palace was erected in Hyde Park without any stone, brick or mortar being used. He had previously designed a gigantic conservatory for Chatsworth House in Derbyshire, and completed his plans for Crystal Palace in only eight days.

New machines and processes

The aim of the Great Exhibition was to show how much industry could help society to progress in peaceful times. Steam power and machines were able to shape and cut metal much faster and more accurately than people ever could. Some machines were giants, such as rolling mills and steam hammers. Others were small and delicate, such as lathes used for turning screw threads or cutting small parts for army rifles.

Progress was hurried along by a series of important inventions and advances in technology. In 1855 the first kind of plastic was made from wood fibres. In 1856 William Perkin produced the first artificial dye (not made from natural materials), which he called 'mauveine'. In the same year Henry Bessemer devised a new method of converting iron ore into steel (a process improved further by William Siemens in 1867). Steel began to be used widely in the expanding shipbuilding industry.

The whole building was 563 metres long and 124 metres wide, and it contained 2.8 kilometres of galleries for the exhibits

The south side of the palace was covered with canvas to keep out the sunlight

The length of the structure was supported by cast-iron beams on top of cast-iron columns

The guttering under the eaves had three grooves — one to catch condensation on the inside, one to hold the glass, and one to catch rain on the outside

The standing figure is echoed by the church tower in the background

There are no signs of an industrial society here, and nothing to date the picture except for the figure's clothing

The photograph is carefully composed, with the reflection of the boatman and pole in the water

The crystal palace

Perhaps the most amazing exhibit at the Great Exhibition was the Crystal Palace itself. Built in less than seven months, it was a bold and revolutionary piece of architecture, like a giant greenhouse made almost entirely of iron and glass. Thackeray described how 'a blazing arch of lucid glass leaps like a fountain from the grass'. It had a framework of iron pieces shaped by machines and lifted into place by huge cranes, and when it was complete it covered an area the size of two football pitches.

◀ A boatman in a punt poses for the camera in Christ Church Meadow near Oxford. The photographer was Charles Lutwidge Dodgson, better known as Lewis Carroll (the author of *Alice in Wonderland*). Dodgson was a keen pioneer of photography, who produced touching portraits of children as well as idyllic country scenes such as this.

Coal and steam, the backbone of the industrial age, became even more valuable. Gas, which was produced when coal was turned into **coke**, was used to light the streets. By the 1880s steam engines were turning dynamos to make electricity, which could then be used to drive factory machines, electric lights and trains on the London underground railway.

Photography

For artists, the development of photography by William Henry Fox Talbot in 1835 had been a curse and a blessing. The camera could reproduce an image far more precisely than a painter or sculptor, but on the other hand it opened up a whole new range of creative possibilities. Interestingly, many **pioneer** photographers used the new technology to look away from the harsh realities of industrial Britain and back to the unspoilt countryside.

Medicine and health

Death's Dispensary, a cartoon from 1866, makes horribly clear that many diseases were spread by filthy water. It shows a street pump being operated by a skeleton, wearing the crown of 'King Cholera'. He pumps water to fill the jugs and buckets of a queue of poor men, women and children, who already look ill from drinking it. Cholera and other deadly diseases such as typhus and dysentery killed as many as 2000 people a week during **epidemics** in the first part of the Victorian age.

The fight against disease

In fact, much had already been done to control disease. In 1848, medical officers had been appointed in every town to make sure the filthy streets were cleaned up. Beginning in 1855, the engineer Joseph Bazalgette had built a new network of pipes under London to supply fresh water, and **sewers** to carry waste away from the city.

Other measures were taken, as officials slowly worked out that epidemics could be controlled. In 1853 the government made it compulsory to **vaccinate** all babies against smallpox (fifty years after the treatment had been discovered). Later, this law was extended to cover vaccination against diphtheria and other diseases. In 1875, councils were given the right to pull down the worst of their germ-ridden **slums**.

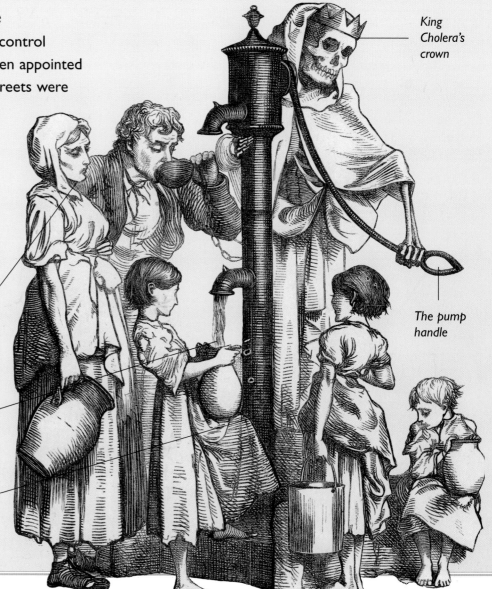

King Cholera's crown

The pump handle

▶ This gruesome cartoon, called *Death's Dispensary*, appeared in a popular magazine with the surprising title of *Fun*.

The Londoners waiting for water have drawn and pale faces

Water gushes out into a jug

Since there were no water taps inside houses, most water came from pumps like this in the street

Victorian hospitals

The architecture of the new Victorian hospitals tells us a great deal about advances in medical care. Until the 1850s, most hospitals were dingy, overcrowded and stuffy places. Buildings such as St Thomas's Hospital in London (completed in 1871) and the Royal Infirmary in Edinburgh (1879) are very different. There are separate wards for patients with different kinds of illnesses, plenty of windows to provide air circulation and light, and bare floors and walls that could be easily cleaned.

This new type of design reflected several vital reforms in Victorian medicine. The most important was the discovery that germs could be passed on by dirty clothing and instruments. In 1871 Joseph Lister introduced an antiseptic acid spray that kept wounds and dressings germ-free. Patients could also be **anaesthetized** – put to sleep – during surgical operations, using the newly developed gas chloroform.

Florence Nightingale

The Crimean Memorial in London contains one statue of a woman – Florence Nightingale by Arthur Walker. There are copies of this work in 10 Downing Street (the British Prime Minister's residence) and St Thomas's Hospital, plus dozens of portraits and photographs in museums and galleries. Florence Nightingale was the most famous woman of the period after the Queen herself. Her deeds during the Crimean War, when she tackled the appalling hospital conditions, made her into the saint-like figure of the famous painting *The Lady with the Lamp*. She later helped reform army medical services and opened the first training school for nurses in 1860.

▶ One of the many portraits of Florence Nightingale. This one, by an unknown artist, hangs in the museum of the Royal Army Medical Corps.

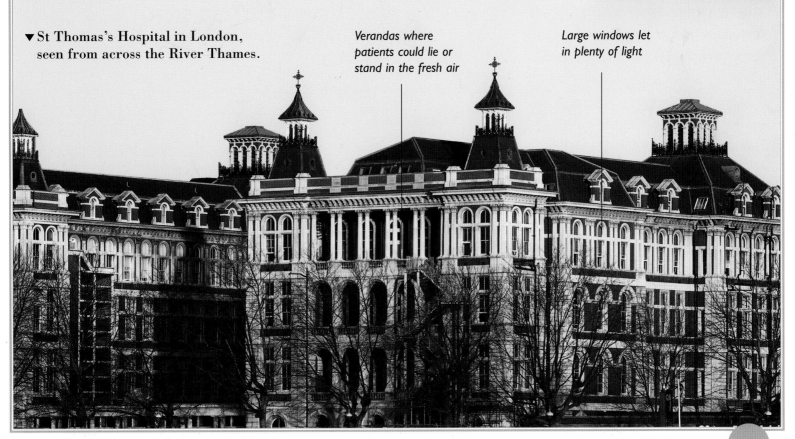

▼ St Thomas's Hospital in London, seen from across the River Thames.

Verandas where patients could lie or stand in the fresh air

Large windows let in plenty of light

Everyday life

Victoria and Albert's royal family was the model for home life in Britain. Between 1840 and 1857 the queen had five daughters and four sons. In private moments she loved to watch the prince playing games with them, although she was determined not to spoil them.

Few other monarchs had ever taken such public delight in their husband and children. This can be seen in several relaxed and happy paintings and **engravings**, as well as the many formal and informal family photographs.

Masters and servants

Countless paintings and photographs show us what an important part the family played in Victorian life. Many of these depict the home life of the growing **middle classes**, with their large, comfortable houses and strict codes of conduct. Everyone had their place. At the head was the father, whose word was obeyed by all without question. The mother looked after the running of the household, while the young children were looked after by a nanny.

▶ Prints like this one hung in many British homes at the end of the Victorian age. It shows scenes from the marriage and family life of Queen Victoria and Prince Albert.

Christ's family

The Victorians saw a happy family life as the foundation of Christian society. Yet when the artist John Everett Millais exhibited his painting *Christ in the House of his Parents* in 1850 he created a scandal. The picture shows Jesus in his father Joseph's workshop surrounded by his loving family, who have wrinkled clothes, dirty fingernails and very ordinary faces. The **realism** of the painting shocked the public, who described it as 'revolting' and 'a nameless atrocity'. They did not want to imagine Jesus living in a normal family.

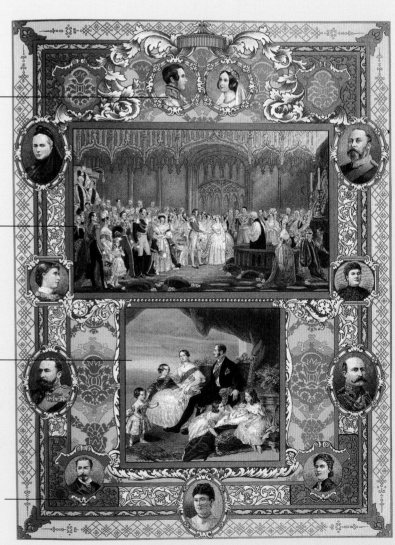

Albert with Victoria at the time of their marriage in 1840

The wedding ceremony of the Queen and Prince Albert

Victoria and Albert with their young children

Portraits of the Queen's children as adults, including the future King Edward VII (top right)

▼ A servant irons laundered clothes with a flat iron, in this 1887 painting by Miss E. D. Herschel.

All the daily work was done by the servants. Wealthy families would have twenty or more servants, including a cook, kitchen maids, housemaids, a butler, a coachman, footmen, gardeners and grooms for the stables. Most working-class households also had one or two servants to cook and clean. Yet very few of them appear in Victorian art. Thomas Woolner's 1893 sculpture *The Housemaid* is a rare exception.

▶ *The Internal Economy of Dotheboys Hall*, one of the hard-hitting illustrations to Charles Dickens's 1838 novel *Nicholas Nickleby*. It was the work of Hablot K. Browne, who used the nickname 'Phiz'. Browne illustrated many of Dickens's finest books.

Victorian children

Rich and poor children had very different lives. In wealthier families, they might see their parents only once a day, just before bedtime. The rest of the time they spent with their nanny in the nursery. Children of poor families probably did not see much of their parents either, because they were expected to work for their living as soon as they were old enough. They might be employed in factories, on street stalls or even as servants in the homes of the rich.

One of the most famous images of Victorian education is the engraving of Dotheboys Hall by Hablot K. Browne, which appeared in Charles Dickens's novel *Nicholas Nickleby*. It is the boarding school of nightmares, where boys were sent to be beaten and starved, well away from their parents. Most fee-paying schools were better than this, of course, but nearly all education cost money. This meant that few British children had any schooling at all. However, after the 1860s several kinds of schools were established by churches and other charities.

Dickens describes the poor pupils of Dotheboys Hall as 'pale and haggard faces, lank and bony figures, children with the countenances of old men'

Wackford Squeers, cruel head of Dotheboys Hall, introduces Nicholas Nickleby to his pupils

Mrs Squeers, the headmaster's terrifying wife

The boys clutch their stomachs after being forced to eat a brimstone and treacle mixture as medicine

Houses and homes

By the 1880s, the rich, the middle classes and the poor lived in different areas. Most industrial towns were dirty, overcrowded and crammed with shops and factories. People who were rich enough moved away from the centres of cities to the quieter 'suburbs' on the edge. From there, they could easily travel to work on the new buses and trains. The very wealthy, as always, built grand houses for themselves further out in the country. This left the poor, who usually had no choice but to stay where they were.

Houses of the upper and middle classes

The massive new country houses, often built by people who had made a fortune in industry, tell us a lot about Victorian pride and morality. They were intended to show off a person's wealth, with ornate decoration and up-to-date home comforts such as gas lighting and running water. The bedrooms of unmarried men and women were kept strictly separate (sometimes with separate staircases).

Suburban houses for the middle classes were larger than those in town centres, with bigger gardens and wider roads. They were usually built in terraces, though more expensive houses were detached. Cheaper housing was also terraced, but even this had attractive features such as carved stone or brick work and bay windows with parapets (low walls along the edge of a roof or balcony).

▼ The main entrance door to the south front of Cragside House in Northumberland. This was a hunting lodge built between 1869 and 1885 to a rambling design by Norman Shaw.

Archaic stone mullions (vertical bars) on the windows

Shaw developed a style that was called Old English. It used features of ancient architecture, such as this medieval type of archway

Houses of the poor

Rural workers had flocked to the factory towns to find work. By 1850, for the first time in British history, more people lived in towns than in the countryside. Employers built cheap housing for them, usually close to their workplace. The houses stood **back-to-back** in bleak double rows with narrow alleys between and no proper drainage. Later houses often had small courtyards containing the toilet and the coal shed.

A few other factory towns tell a different story. In 1850, the **textile manufacturer** Sir Titus Salt moved his works out of Bradford in Yorkshire and built Saltaire, a new town in the open countryside. It provided well-designed and pleasant surroundings for his workers. He realized that people worked better if they were happy and healthy. Other employers followed Salt's example, notably soap manufacturer William Lever, who began building Port Sunlight in Merseyside in 1888, and George Cadbury who founded a 'model village' near his chocolate factory in Birmingham in 1893.

▼ Norman Shaw's design for the Old Swan House on Chelsea Embankment in London, drawn in 1876.

▲ A colourful advertisement for Sunlight soap, produced at Port Sunlight in Merseyside.

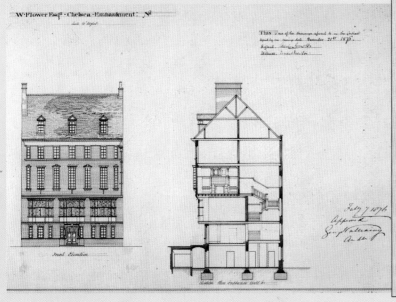

Great architects

Joseph Paxton (1801–65) began his career as a gardener's boy. He later designed huge greenhouses for Chatsworth House in Derbyshire and was chosen as architect of the revolutionary metal and glass structure of the Crystal Palace in 1851.

George Gilbert Scott (1811–78) is best known for the many churches he built in the style of the **Gothic Revival**. He also designed several London landmarks, including the Albert Memorial, the Foreign Office and the St Pancras Hotel.

Charles Rennie Mackintosh (1868–1928) was a Scottish architect and **pioneer** of the Modern Movement in art. His most famous work was the 1899 School of Art in Glasgow, with its huge studio windows and plain stonework.

Design and craft

The industrial revolution had made it possible for all sorts of objects, from pins to steamships, to be produced quickly and cheaply. The Great Exhibition of 1851 had celebrated this speed and power. A network of Schools of Design was set up, where boys could learn how to draw plans and put art to the practical use of helping industry. The schools taught strict rules about such things as decoration and style, and did not encourage imaginative ideas.

Morris and Company

Not everyone welcomed the new age of machine-made things. Some saw that the factory system was depriving people of pride and pleasure in their work, and producing poor-quality goods. Among the fiercest critics of industry was William Morris, who wrote: 'It is not this or that machine which we want to get rid of, but the great machine of commercial tyranny which oppresses [saddens and damages] the lives of us all.'

A poet, designer and trained architect, Morris was also a **socialist** who hated industrial civilization. He believed that it was robbing people of their traditional craft skills, and creating objects which were badly designed. He longed for a return to the values and standards of the guilds (associations of tradespeople) of medieval times, when goods were made by hand. In 1861 he founded a company to manufacture carpets, wallpaper, stained glass and furniture, later to be known as Morris and Company.

▼ A wall hanging designed by William Morris and embroidered with crewel, a thin woollen yarn used for tapestry.

The main motifs are of artichokes. Much of Morris's inspiration came from natural things such as birds and plants

Border influenced by Persian and Indian textile designs

The main designs are interspersed with tendrils, leaves and other plant decorations

Morris made sure that the materials used in his products (such as the crewels) were coloured with the best and most exact dyes

The Arts and Crafts Movement

Morris and his colleagues described themselves as 'Fine Art Workmen in Painting, Carving, Furniture and the Metals'. They had great success, and were commissioned to redecorate the interiors at St James's Palace and the South Kensington Museum in London. William Morris wallpaper and textiles are still popular now. His most important achievement, however, was to inspire what became known as the Arts and Crafts Movement.

This was not an organized association, but a varied collection of artists and designers who aimed to produce articles in an 'honest' way. The products had to show openly what kind of materials they were made of and how they worked, without pretending to be something else. Among the most notable members of the movement was William de Morgan, who made magnificent pottery using medieval methods, and the architect Charles Rennie Mackintosh, who designed startling wooden furniture.

▶ Several painters reacted against what they saw as the fussy detail of Pre-Raphaelite painting. One of these was Frederick Walker, whose 1865 picture *Autumn* is shown here. He produced a dreamy effect by painting in the details and then partly rubbing them out. The still and carefully posed position of the girl, and the symbolic apple in her hand, suggest the melancholy aspect of autumn and the ending of summer.

The Pre-Raphaelites

William Morris was closely linked to a revolutionary new movement in painting launched in 1848. It was formed by a group of artists, including John Everett Millais, William Holman Hunt and Dante Gabriel Rossetti, who called themselves 'The **Pre-Raphaelite** Brotherhood'. They rejected what they saw as the artificial style taught by art schools such as the Royal Academy, and returned to the values of medieval painters. Pre-Raphaelite means 'before the time of Raphael' (an influential Italian Renaissance painter). The brotherhood caused a sensation with the glowing colours and natural figures in their pictures.

Life in the country

The early Victorian age was a boom time for British farmers. Improved methods of growing crops and raising livestock produced much more food. This was eagerly snapped up the people of the rapidly expanding new industrial towns: prices rocketed, and farmers sold all they could grow. By 1875 the boom was over. There were disastrous harvests and plagues of disease that destroyed vast numbers of cattle and sheep. Cheaper imported food began to flood in from the USA, Argentina and Australia. Many farmers were ruined, and poverty and hardship became widespread in rural areas.

Art and reality

The vast majority of Victorian paintings of the countryside show us a rosy, peaceful and innocent world. There are sturdy farm workers in smocks, harvesters sleeping under haystacks, thatched cottages with pretty gardens, cosy village schools, cart-horses standing in streams and dramatic hunting scenes. Artists often used picturesque rustic settings for their moral pictures, such as Ford Madox Brown's *The Hireling Shepherd* and *Strayed Sheep*.

The British countryside was still a beautiful place, but life for the average farm labourer was usually very different from what we can see in these works. They lived in rented cottages that were small, dark and damp, and ate mostly root vegetables and fatty bacon. They worked long and backbreaking hours out of doors in all weathers, though sometimes in winter work was scarce. If they lost their jobs, they lost their pitiful wages and home at the same time, and had to live in the local **workhouse**.

▼ Ford Madox Brown often used echoes of Bible stories in his paintings to make a moral point. This one, *The Hireling Shepherd*, was painted in 1852 and features a finely detailed and idyllic country setting.

The sheep begin to stray. One is about to go into the cornfield

The shepherd has been hired, so the sheep do not belong to him. He cares more for kissing the girls than he does for his flock

The shepherd shows her a butterfly he has caught

The girl nurses a baby lamb on her lap

Paradise lost

Why did so many artists concentrate on the idyllic side of rural life? The obvious reason is that the people who bought their paintings wanted something pretty and cheering. Perhaps the painters also believed that they were preserving a part of the British landscape which was changing rapidly. The traditional country dweller was disappearing (the number of farm workers fell from 1.3 million in 1851 to 0.7 million in 1901), as jobless people went to find work in towns. Steam ploughs, steam **threshers** and mechanical **reapers** were replacing many of the old agricultural skills.

Of course, there were some painters who depicted the darker reality of poverty and despair. Henry Wallis's *The **Stonebreaker*** of 1858 shows a workman who has died on his stone heap. George Clausen's *Bird Scaring* of 1896 shows a ragged boy with a sack round his shoulders driving crows from a cornfield. Few, however, were brave enough to challenge popular taste in this way.

▼ A model farm built by wealthy landowners, with a large farmhouse and tithe barn, at Bradford-on-Avon in Wiltshire, 1878.

The model farm

A few wealthy and forward-looking farmers used modern architectural design and building methods to create brand-new 'model farms'. These included planned farmyards surrounded by hygienic and spacious milking parlours, cowsheds, dairies and other facilities. The buildings were sometimes even decorated with carvings, cast-ironwork and other features.

▼ Some of the harsh realities of Victorian country life are captured by George Clausen in his 1896 picture *Bird Scaring*.

The boy shakes wooden clappers to scare away the crows and other birds who might steal the newly sown seed from the ploughed field

He has lit a fire to give a little warmth on this bleak winter day

The boy is shouting. Is he simply driving away the birds? Or is he trying to call to someone in another field?

The small boy is the only figure, emphasizing the loneliness of the job

Entertainment

In spite of its horrors, the industrial age gave ordinary people time to relax. Most of them earned more money and worked shorter hours than ever before in British history. The term 'week-end' was invented in the 1870s, because this was when people first had more than one day off at the end of the working week. The extra free time gave them the chance to enjoy their leisure, and encouraged the growth of many new pastimes.

▼ The countryside is the main subject in this view of a village cricket match near Gravesend, painted in about 1830.

Fun and games

As education improved, more Britons could read, and there was a huge demand for popular fiction and magazines. Even poets, such as Lord Tennyson, became bestsellers. However, most working men liked to go out on a Saturday evening (women, especially wives, usually stayed at home). The best-loved entertainment was at the theatre, where people could see everything from thrilling **melodramas** to the variety turns of the **music hall**. Paintings and sketches by artists such as Richard Doyle and Walter Sickert show the raucous and smoky atmosphere inside such places.

▶ Summer holidays on the beach were invented by the Victorians. William Powell Frith's *Life at the Seaside (Ramsgate Sands)* gives a vivid picture of this new kind of enjoyment. The realism, the modern setting and the depiction of many different classes grouped together shocked some critics.

A little girl paddles at the water's edge

A man gives a Punch and Judy Show

Some people go on donkey rides

The barbaric old sports such as cock-fighting and badger-baiting were banned, and organized activities took their place. Thousands of people turned out every weekend to take part in football and cricket as well as newer pastimes such as cycling, lawn tennis and even roller-skating. The Football Association was founded in 1863 and the English Rugby Union in 1871, while the first cricket Test Match between England and Australia was played in 1877.

Going on holiday

Victorian artists liked to paint big, crowded scenes with plenty of action and detail. The new leisure activity of going on holiday excursions provided a perfect subject. William Powell Frith's *Life at the Seaside* (1854) depicts hordes of people on Ramsgate sands, happy to be playing, paddling, riding donkeys or just marvelling at the sea. *Boulter's Lock – Sunday Afternoon* by Edward Gregory (1897) is another highly detailed picture, showing Londoners boating on the Thames.

These paintings and many others (such as Frith's panorama of race crowds on Derby Day) invite us to ask questions. For example, how did all these people get there? Most probably they used the rapidly improving (and still cheap) public transport of trams, buses and trains. What kind of people are they? A close look at the clothes and other details suggest that these are holidaymakers of all classes mingling together, though they still seem to dress very formally – especially at the seaside.

Parks and gardens

The Victorians loved gardens and gardening, for the new terraced houses often had small garden plots behind. Everyone could walk in the many new public parks and ornamental gardens that were opened in this period in many large towns. Apart from the plants, these contained many decorative features, from bandstands and giant conservatories (glass rooms for protecting plants) to ponds and fountains.

Religion and society

Victorians believed that they were deeply religious. So the results of the 1851 countrywide **census** came as a shock. This survey showed that fewer than half of the British population of 18 million actually went to religious services. Only about 3 million of them belonged to the Church of England.

The Church of England was seen by many as the faith of the wealthy and the **middle classes**. Most vicars came from the upper sections of society and many had little in common with the people who attended their churches.

▼ William Holman Hunt visited the lands of the Bible many times. His symbolic painting *The Scapegoat* (1854) was one of the most famous religious pictures of the age.

Christian teachings

Even so, Christianity, and the Church of England in particular, had an enormous influence on the lives of British people. They accepted that moral standards had been set by church leaders from the teachings of the Bible, which was seen as the direct word of God. Therefore anyone who questioned or disobeyed these rules was also disobeying God. Obedience to authority (meaning teachers, priests and parents) was the first duty taught to children.

The scapegoat was an animal traditionally turned out into the desert to die. It took with it all the sins of the Israelites

The desolate and barren shores around the Dead Sea

Bones of other animals that have died here

The horns are an echo of the Cross, linking the goat with the death of Jesus

Plinth at the base, decorated with relief carvings

Seated statue of Prince Albert inside

Fluted columns support the roof

▲ The incredibly ornate Memorial for Prince Albert, in Kensington Gardens in London. It was designed by George Gilbert Scott in the ornamented style of the **Gothic Revival** and completed in 1875.

Christianity in art

Many Victorian paintings had a directly Christian message, even ones that seem to be about doubt and despair. *The Doubt: 'Can these Dry Bones Live?'*, painted by Henry Alexander Bowler in 1855, is a clear example. It shows a woman leaning on a churchyard gravestone, staring at a skull and bones that have come to the surface of the soil. Seeing these, how was it possible to believe in life after death? Yet there are plenty of clues in the picture that answer the question in the title.

▶ *The Doubt: 'Can these Dry Bones Live?'* is a small canvas (61 × 51 centimetres), but it asks many of the religious questions that troubled the mid-Victorians. The artist firmly believed in life after death. The inscription on the tomb of 'John Faithful' reads 'I am the Resurrection and the Life'. A butterfly (the corpse's soul?) sits on the skull.

Death was also a very obvious presence. Many people still died young – from disease, hunger or violence – and funerals and gravestones were all too familiar to most. The threat of death can be seen from the many paintings of graveyard scenes, which show grieving widows, sobbing mothers and the burials of babies. There are hundreds of ornate and dramatic Victorian tombs and memorials, notably royal ones such as the tomb of the Duke of Clarence at Windsor.

Church and chapel

One result of the 1851 census findings was to drive ahead religious reform. Alternative kinds of Christianity became widely popular because they tried to reach out to those who shunned the church, especially the urban poor. The Evangelicals organized charities and shelters in London and industrial towns, and grew into a major force in Victorian Britain. They taught the belief that all people were sinners, and could only be saved from Hell by being sorry for their sins and leading a strict moral life.

Other Christian groups outside the Church of England (generally called Nonconformists) attracted working-class people. These included the Methodists and the Baptists, who worshipped in their own chapels that were much barer and simpler than traditional churches. All the same, Victorian church services were long and solemn. The parson's sermon alone might last over an hour – and many families went two or even three times every Sunday.

Stories in paintings

'Telling the tale of a life on a single canvas' was how one artist described narrative painting in 1868. This style of picture, crowded with details and action, became extremely popular in Victorian Britain. It was an age in which people loved stories, and made bestsellers of the enthralling novels of Charles Dickens, Wilkie Collins, Mrs Humphry Ward and Robert Louis Stevenson. So it was natural that pictures which told stories should be in great demand too – rather like TV soaps are today.

What kinds of stories?

In previous times, narrative paintings had often featured grand and important stories such as battles and other public events. The Victorians preferred simpler and more personal tales, often set in people's homes, or in harvest fields, or village streets. Many earlier pictures showed charming little incidents, such as William Mulready's *The Last In*, in which a schoolboy tries to slip unnoticed into class. Others, such as William Powell Frith's *Derby Day*, were massive canvases packed with characters and events.

▼ Many of the paintings of Henry La Thangue tell a powerful story even though they are often static and concentrate on a few apparently ordinary figures. *The Last Furrow*, from 1895, is a moving portrait of a dying man, set in a realistic everyday situation.

The artist shows the straight and true furrows he has already cut – perhaps signifying his upright life

A horse looks round to see what has happened

One handle of the plough supports his body as he falls

He still clutches the reins

The labourer has completed the last furrow as he ploughs the field, then collapses

► In contrast to La Thangue's painting, George Smith's equally tragic picture *The Soldier's Wife* is packed with detail. The painting shows the effect of news of foreign wars reaching home – a very popular subject, especially with so many soldiers fighting in remote parts of the British Empire.

A print showing the Duke of Wellington, a famous British military leader

The husband's empty chair

The eldest daughter looks fearfully at her mother

The newspaper with the account of his death lies crumpled on the floor

The wife weeps after learning of her husband's death far away

The three younger children do not realize what has happened. They carry on with their game of toy soldiers – an ironic echo of the real bloodshed

Later pictures tended to teach lessons. There are countless narratives concerning early death (especially in childhood), and the receiving of bad news from soldiers or sailors abroad. There are paintings about immoral behaviour, such as love affairs outside marriage or pregnant girls being thrown out of their homes. Unhappy marriages and wasted fortunes are other common themes.

Reading a picture

Artists expected viewers to look long and closely at their paintings. They needed time to follow the narrative, work out the relationships between the characters and understand the various clues and symbols that might be included. For instance, *The Man with the Scythe* by Henry La Thangue (1896) looks like a simple and ordinary scene, but contains a much darker meaning once it is examined carefully.

Narrative paintings obviously give us an enormous amount of practical information about how the Victorians lived. *The Volunteers* by Arthur Boyd Houghton (1861) is rich in details of the clothing (including the uniforms of the volunteer soldiers themselves) and manners of the subjects. Indoor scenes such as *The Soldier's Wife* by George Smith (1878) show furniture, toys, pots and pans and dozens of other daily objects.

Missionaries and explorers

Even in the mid-19th century, there were many parts of the world where Europeans had never been. Hundreds of Victorian travellers set off for remote or little-known places in Africa, Asia and South America. Some went for trade, to secure new territories (often in newly conquered parts of the British Empire), raw materials or goods. Others went out of curiosity, to explore or answer age-old questions. There were also travellers who went as **missionaries** to convert people to Christianity.

Out of Africa

A few of these Christian missionaries became great explorers as well. The most famous was David Livingstone, a Scottish doctor who spent many years in Africa campaigning against slavery and establishing mission stations (where missionaries held religious services and gave medical aid to local people). He was one of several British adventurers who helped to show that the mighty River Nile flowed out of the lake now called Victoria Nyanza. Livingstone's exploits (and the news picture of his sensational meeting with H. M. Stanley in 1871) did much to inspire British fascination with Africa.

▶ A strangely modern-looking portrait of Mutesa, the King of Buganda in Africa. It was painted by Dorothy Stanley, the wife of H. M. Stanley, who explored the Congo River and other parts of central Africa. She copied it from a photograph.

Travellers discovered many wonderful things in Africa. Amazing new animals were pictured (and sometimes brought back and housed in zoos), including the gorilla, the zebra and the hyena. Mary Kingsley tramped through the bush and swamps of west Africa in her long skirt and high-necked blouse, carrying an umbrella. She brought back fascinating insights into the lives of the feared Fang people. Of course, many treasures were seized by brute force. When British troops conquered Benin, western Africa, in 1897, they looted the capital city and stole priceless bronze works of art, which remain in the British Museum in London.

He wears a tarbush cap (cap with a tassel but no brim) on his head

He stares at the viewer with large, restless eyes. His expression is described as 'nervous but expressive of intelligence'

Mutesa is tall and slim

The walls of Mutesa's compound (settlement)

▶ *The North-West Passage* by John Everett Millais was painted in 1874, just when a new expedition was setting out. It sold for the enormous sum of £4700.

Edward Lear

Edward Lear is best known today as a writer of nonsense poems such as 'The Owl and the Pussycat'. He was also a superb landscape painter. His watercolours, painted quickly on the spot, record sights on his many journeys through the Mediterranean and to places as distant as Egypt and India.

A portrait of Horatio Nelson, England's great naval hero

A glimpse of the sea, with a sailing ship in the distance

The Union Jack and the White Ensign (a naval flag) are proudly hung from the walls

Navigators and naturalists

By the 1870s it seemed as if Britain could conquer the whole world. This is reflected in paintings such as *The North-West Passage* by John Everett Millais, which celebrated a new voyage to find a sea passage round the far north of America. Several previous expeditions had failed (notably the one led by John Franklin in 1845, which simply disappeared in the icy wastes). Even so, the artist's sub-title is optimistic – 'It might be done: and England should do it'. The picture is not of ships or the sea, but of the leader's wife and ageing father left behind, poring over maps.

More exotic images came back from South America. Beginning in 1848 the scientists Henry Bates and Alfred Wallace travelled up the Amazon River by boat, collecting specimens of animals and plants. Bates alone gathered over 14,000 different kinds of insect, which he shipped back to England. Exquisite pictures of many of these new species were painted by artists such as John Gould.

▼ This picture has the sub-title *Painting of Hitherto Unknown Animals*, although these creatures look fairly familiar today. It is an illustration from a book describing the natural history of the animal kingdom published in 1847. Artists took great delight in painting these unusual and exotic new discoveries.

The chamois or mountain goat

The gazelle, of which many kinds were found in Africa

The giraffe, which early explorers hunted with dogs

A giraffe using its long neck to reach foliage high up in a tree

Darwin and doubt

'Man is descended from a hairy, tailed quadruped [animal with four feet], probably arboreal [tree-dwelling] in its habits.' With these words Charles Darwin introduced a major work explaining his theories of evolution, *The Descent of Man*, in 1871. This followed the 1859 publication of his first book *The Origin of Species*, which had already caused a storm of outrage and controversy among traditional churchgoers. Darwin suggested that humans had evolved (changed gradually) from ape-like creatures over millions of years.

Science versus religion

Darwin's theories seemed to undermine the authority of the Bible itself. If evolution had taken so long, then God could not possibly have created the world and everything in it within a few days. If animals went on evolving, then God could not have made them perfect in the first place. These and other doubts led many people to question the teachings of Christianity.

Others angrily made fun of Darwin for suggesting that they were related to monkeys. Some of the most famous images of the time are cartoons which show him with an ape's body, or even perched up in a tree. A great debate took place at Oxford in 1860, in which a well-known bishop attacked the idea of evolution but was made to look ridiculous by one of Darwin's supporters. No one would have dared to challenge a religious leader in this way in the early years of Victoria's reign.

▼ Charles Darwin is shown with an ape's body in this cartoon from the *Hornet* magazine, drawn at the height of the evolution debate. It is entitled 'A Venerable Orang-utan'.

Darwin's head, with eyebrows, nose and ears distorted to look more monkey-like

An ape's body, shown crouching on the forest floor

▶ *Hope*, by George Frederic Watts. He was not a conventional Christian, and this picture has nothing to do with the Bible. The figure of Hope was intended to inspire people whatever their religion.

Late Victorians

The shock of Darwinism helped to change the atmosphere of the last years of the Victorian era. The wonderful advances and discoveries of science no longer seemed to demonstrate the power of an all-knowing God – in fact they seemed to show the opposite. A division grew up between religion and science. People were less certain about what they believed. The empire might be getting even bigger, but there were signs that Britain's top position in the world was under threat from growing nations such as the USA and Germany.

This darker and less certain mood can be seen in some of the work of late Victorian artists. George Frederic Watts had painted many religious subjects during his long life, but in 1886 he produced *Hope*. This picture contained no Christian symbols. Instead it featured a blindfolded woman (representing Hope) sitting on a globe and playing a lyre with broken strings.

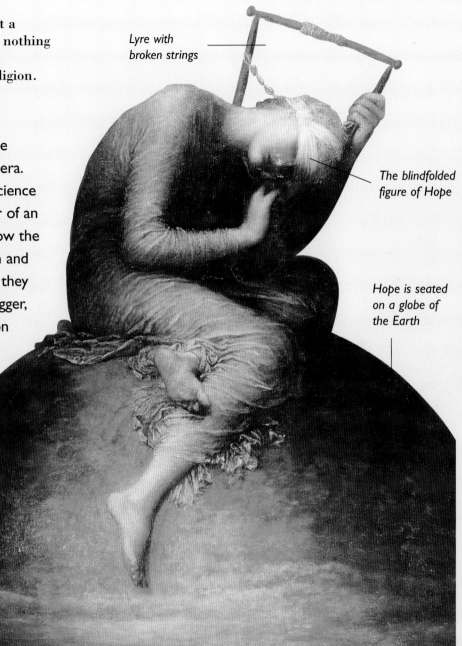

Lyre with broken strings

The blindfolded figure of Hope

Hope is seated on a globe of the Earth

▶ The Dinosaur Hall of the Natural History Museum in London, with its famous skeletons.

A museum for natural history

Some of the most stunning of all Victorian buildings are the museums created to display the discoveries and products of the age. The most famous of these is the Natural History Museum in London, designed by Alfred Waterhouse and completed in 1881. Its huge central hall, soaring towers and rich decoration reflected the massive surge of interest in the natural world during this period.

Timeline

Early Victorian Period

1837
Victoria comes to the throne on the death of her uncle William IV

1838
Chartists launch their campaign for wider voting rights
Charles Dickens publishes *Oliver Twist*

1839
W. H. Fox Talbot first publishes the explanation of his photography work

1840
Victoria marries Prince Albert; Penny Post introduced

1841
Great Western Railway links London and Bristol

1842
Edwin Chadwick's Poor Law Report on the conditions of poor people

1844
Laws passed to limit working hours of women and children

1845
Potato blight begins long famine in Ireland

1846
Edwin Chadwick publishes damning report on urban poverty

1847
The 'Ten-Hour' Act further limits working hours

1849
Cholera **epidemic** kills 2000 a week throughout Britain

1851
The Great Exhibition opens at Crystal Palace, London

Mid-Victorian Period

1853–56
War in the Crimea against Russia

1855
David Livingstone is the first European to see the Victoria Falls in Southern Africa

c.1855
Alexander Parkes develops first plastic from wood fibres

1856
William Perkin makes first artificial dye; Henry Bessemer invents new **steel**-making process

1857
Rebellion in India against British rule

1859
Charles Darwin publishes *The Origin of Species*; the **Pre-Raphaelite** Brotherhood is formed

1860
Florence Nightingale opens the first nursing school in London

1861
Death of Prince Albert

1863
London's first underground railway opens

1866
Brunel's ship *Great Eastern* lays telegraph cables across the Atlantic

1867
Second Reform Act allows more men to vote in general elections; Fenian revolution in Ireland

1869
Suez Canal opens between Mediterranean and Red Sea

1870
Education Act makes the government responsible for setting up elementary (primary) schools; **Home Rule** Party founded in Ireland

1871
Joseph Lister introduces antiseptic spray to hospital surgery

Late Victorian Period

1876
Alexander Graham Bell invents the telephone; Queen Victoria becomes Empress of India

1878
William Booth founds the Salvation Army

1880
New law makes school compulsory for children between ages five and ten

1882
First electricity generating stations built

1883–98
War in the Sudan

1887
Riots in Ireland over the issue of Home Rule; Conan Doyle publishes first Sherlock Holmes story

1888
Scottish Labour Party founded by Keir Hardie

1889
All-out strike paralyses London docks

1893
George Cadbury begins building model village for workers near Birmingham

1894
Manchester Ship Canal opens

1897
Victoria's Diamond Jubilee

1899–1902
Boer War in South Africa

1901
Death of Queen Victoria

Glossary

abstract not representing things in a realistic way, but expressing the artist's ideas about them

anaesthetic drug that puts patients to sleep or numbs an area of the body before an operation

back-to-back houses double row of houses joined at the back but facing opposite ways

census official count or recording of population figures

Chartism campaign to fight for political equality, especially the right to vote

coke black substance that is produced from coal and burnt to provide heat

colony land conquered or settled by people from a foreign country and then ruled from that country

engraving picture or decoration made by carving or etching (burning with acid) on a block or plate of material

epidemic rapid and wide spread of a disease among people

garrison post or stronghold where soldiers are stationed

Gothic Revival the return to the style of medieval architecture

Home Rule government of a country by its own inhabitants, instead of being governed from abroad

Impressionists artists who attempted to paint a scene by giving a general impression of it rather than an exact and detailed one

lathe machine that turns a piece of metal or wood, allowing it to be evenly shaped with tools

manufacturers people or organizations that make goods

melodrama play full of suspense and sensational events, with a happy ending

middle class class of people between the upper class and the working class, which grew rapidly during the Victorian age

missionary person who goes to a foreign country to promote his or her religious faith

music hall show made up of singing, dancing and comedy acts

petition document with many signatures asking for action on a particular matter

pioneer someone who goes into new territory or creates something new in the fields of science or invention

pollution the harming of the environment with poisons or other dangerous substances

Pre-Raphaelite member of a group of 19th-century artists who painted in a style similar to 14th- and 15th-century Italian artists

realism showing things as they really are rather than making them look better, as many Victorian artists did

reaper machine that cuts down and gathers crops

sewer underground drain for carrying away dirty water

slum urban area that is overcrowded and where people live in squalid conditions and poor housing

socialist person who believes that political power and the means of making and selling goods should be shared between everyone in society

steel strong and easily shaped metal made of a mixture of iron and carbon

stonebreaker worker who breaks up large rocks so that the pieces can be used to patch roads

textile cloth made by weaving

thresher machine that separates the grains of corn from the ears (stalks and husks)

trade union association of workers in a particular trade or profession

vaccinate inject a person with a mild form of a disease so they will be able to fight it off if they come into contact with it

workhouse public hostel where local people in poverty were fed and housed

Further resources

Books

British History: The Victorian Age 1837–1914 (Kingfisher, 2002)

Callow, Simon, ***Dickens' Christmas: A Victorian Celebration*** (Assorted, 2003)

Ellis, Roger, ***Who's Who in Victorian Britain*** (Shepheard-Walwyn, 1997)

Lambourne, Lionel, ***Victorian Painting*** (Phaidon Press, 2003)

Malam, John, and Antram, David, ***You Wouldn't Want to be a Victorian Schoolchild*** (Hodder Children's Books, 2002)

Scott, Colin, ***Victorian Transport*** (Hodder Children's Books, 2003)

Websites

http://www.britainexpress.com/History/Victorian_index.htm Information about Victorian life, including art and architecture

www.history.ac.uk/ihr/Focus/Victorian General information about the Victorian era

http://www.bbc.co.uk/history/lj/victorian_britainlj/index.shtml Historical evidence from cartoons and novels

www.victorian-art.com Victorian oil paintings

www.victorianart.btinternet.co.uk Victorian art and design

www.victorianartinbritain.co.uk Pre-Raphaelite and other Victorian art

www.victorianweb.org/art Victorian art, fashion and costume

Places to visit

Bristol
Clifton Suspension Bridge
SS *Great Britain*

Cardiff
Cardiff Castle
Welsh Industrial and Maritime
  Museum

County Durham
North of England Open Air Musem

County Tyrone
The Argory

Derbyshire
Calke Abbey

Edinburgh
Museum of Childhood
Royal Museum of Scotland

Glasgow
Art School
St Andrew's Halls

Isle of Wight
Osborne House

Kent
The Red House, Bexleyheath

Leeds
Town Hall

Liverpool
Albert Dock
Port Sunlight
Stanley Park

London
Buckingham Palace
Houses of Parliament

London (continued)
Kew Gardens
Natural History Museum
St Pancras station
Tate Britain
Victoria and Albert Museum

Manchester
Free Trade Hall

Oxford
Pitt-Rivers Museum
University Museum

Somerset
Tyntesfield House

York
Castle Museum
National Railway Museum

Index

Titles in the *History in Art* series include:

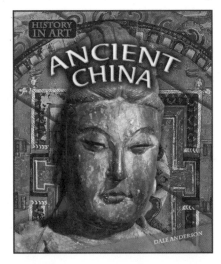

Hardback   1 844 43369 2

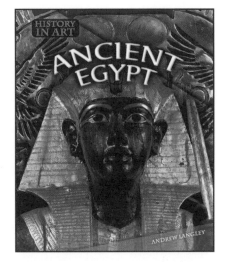

Hardback   1 844 43361 7

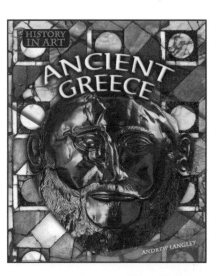

Hardback   1 844 43359 5

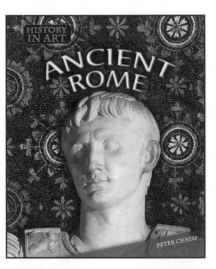

Hardback   1 844 43360 9

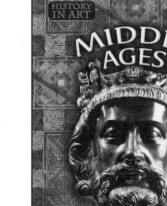

Hardback   1 844 43362 5

Hardback   1 844 43370 6

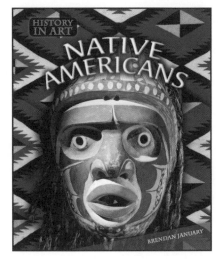

Hardback   1 844 43371 4

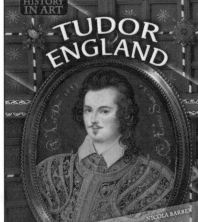

Hardback   1 844 43372 2

Hardback   1 844 43373 0

Find out about the other titles in this series on our website www.raintreepublishers.co.uk

These Chinese children live in the snowy Tibetan Plateau. They are wearing layers of clothes to keep themselves warm. They include vests, T-shirts, jumpers and coats.

Bits and bobs

People all over the world enjoy wearing jewellery. Indian women may wear nose rings and earrings.

In Hawaii children decorate their hair and make necklaces using flowers.

This girl comes from the Guizhou Province in China. She is wearing silver necklaces and decorations in her hair.

Sportswear

Some baseball players wear a special helmet and gloves to protect themselves from the hard ball.

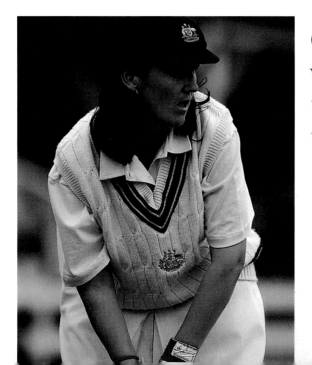

Cricketers usually wear white clothes, because they show up well against the green grass.

Surfers wear special suits which keep their bodies warm when they spend a long time in the water.

Ice hockey is a fast game. The players wear helmets and padded clothing to protect themselves from the ice and from contact with other players.

29

Glossary

anorak A warm waterproof coat.

carnival A festival when people enjoy themselves.

embroidered Decorated with fancy stitches.

fustanella A white, knee-length skirt worn by men in Greece.

kilt A knee-length, pleated skirt.

Morris dancers English dancers who usually perform with sticks and bells.

sunscreen Cream which protects the skin from burning.

thermal Warm.

wet suits Tight rubber suits which keep swimmers and surfers warm in the cold water.

Books to read

Children's Clothes by Miriam Moss (Wayland, 1988)

Just Look at Clothes by Ralph Lewis
    (Macdonald Educational, 1986)

The Usborne Book of World Geography (Usborne, 1993)

Focus on Japan by Pilbeam (Hamish Hamilton, 1987)

Focus on Greece by Dicks (Hamish Hamilton, 1988)

More information

Would you like to know about the people and places you have seen in the photographs in this book? If so, read on.

pages 4–5
Girl dressed in T-shirt and shorts, pictured with Pluto at Disney World in Florida. Florida is on the south-east coast of the USA and the weather is warm all year round.
Children at a market in Dien Bien Phu, Taiwan. Taiwan is an island off the south-east coast of China.
Canadian Indian boy dressed in clothes made from animal skins to keep warm.
Little Tibetan boy dressed in warm clothes. Tibet is a high mountainous region of south-west China.

pages 6–7
Man wearing a sunhat at a cricket match in Sydney, Australia.
Women embroidering patterns on to material in the village of Ile Los Urus in Peru. Peru is on the west coast of South America.
Yarmulkes are worn during prayer by very religious Jewish boys and men.

pages 8–9
These women are from Rajasthan in northern India. They are wearing saris, the traditional dress of women from India and Pakistan. A sari is a long piece of coloured material which is wrapped around the body.
Trainers are worn not only for sport, but for fashion and comfort too.

pages 10–11
Norway is a country in northern Europe. Winters are very cold in Norway; the country is covered with snow and ice for many months. People have to dress up warmly.
Children in the Gassim region of Saudi Arabia. People in hot countries often wear white clothes because the colour reflects heat. This means that the heat is thrown back.
Vietnam is a country in South-East Asia.

pages 12–13
Thermal material traps heat.
Gym class at a school in north London, England.

pages 14–15
Babygros have popper buttons along each leg and across the bottom to make it easy to change the baby's nappy.
Parents have always carried their babies in slings or backpacks. Babies find it very comfortable and it leaves the carrier's hands free to carry shopping or to do some gardening, for example.
This Guatemalan mother is able to shop at the market while carrying her baby in a shawl.

pages 16–17
At the Dragon Boat festival, boats decorated with dragons' heads are raced.
Indonesia is a group of over 3000 small islands in South-East Asia.
These women are wearing the traditional Japanese kimono as part of the Hollyhock festival.

pages 18–19
The traditional costume of Peru.
Soldiers guarding the Tomb of the Unknown Soldier in Athens, Greece.

pages 20–21
Taking part in the Retro carnival in Cologne, Germany.
This magnificent costume was worn during carnival time in Port of Spain, Trinidad.
Morris dancers in Yorkshire, England. The dancers dress up to celebrate spring.

pages 22–23
Keeping cool at the seaside in shorts.
It is very important to wear sunscreen when you go out in strong sunshine. Sunscreen comes in different strengths, to suit all types of skin.
These Saudi Arabian women follow the Muslim religion. They have covered themselves up as part of their religious beliefs.

pages 24–25
Quebec is in the east of Canada. The winter is bitterly cold, so it is important to wear clothes made from warm materials.
Lapland is an area of northern Europe. People who live there wear clothes made from reindeer skin to protect them from the ice-cold weather.
The weather in China is extreme; it is freezing cold in the north and sub-tropical in the south of the country.

pages 26–27
Running along a beautiful Hawaiian beach. Hawaii is part of the USA; it is an island off the west coast, in the Pacific Ocean.
Chinese girl wearing jewellery and clothes which are traditional to the region she comes from.

pages 28–29
Behind the player with the bat sits the catcher, and behind the catcher crouches the umpire, in this game of baseball.
Julie Calvert batting for the Australian women's cricket team.
Surfers testing the waves on Bondi Beach in Sydney, Australia.
Ice hockey is played by two teams of six players.

31

Index